THE ESSENCE OF RAISING CHILDREN

*Conscious Parenting, Habits, and Emotional
Health to Shape the Heart of Our Children*

Rosalina Rangel

I dedicate this book
to my sons:

They help me grow every day,
they strengthen me,
they brighten my life with their little surprises
and remind me
that life has so much more to offer.

Juan José and Samuel Pinto

An Invitation to the Table

Welcome to this space, created especially for you. If this book has found its way into your hands, it is because your heart holds a deep desire to guide your children's lives with wisdom and purpose. Before we begin exploring the tools that psychology and science offer us, I invite you to pause for a moment and breathe with a sense of calm. Motherhood is often presented as a pursuit of perfection, but here we will discover a far more comforting truth: the true goal is presence. What your children truly need in order to grow with security is your willingness to be by their side, nurturing the unique bond that only the two of you share.

Our love, just as it is today, is the strongest foundation upon which they build their world. You carry within you the essential resources for this journey. Your experience, your devotion, and your daily intention are valuable gifts that arise from the abundance of what you are already sowing with care.

Throughout these pages, we will explore habits, boundaries, and principles of emotional health with the confidence that this journey moves in a clear and hopeful direction, where today's consistency becomes tomorrow's security.

As we move forward together, you will discover that the maturity of your path gradually reveals a deeper quality of relationship. Every step taken today becomes a seed of joy that grows richer and sweeter with time. Under the blessing of grace, the most beautiful chapters of your story are already being prepared today.

Rosalina Rangel

TABLE OF CONTENTS

Chapter 1

Being a Mom Is Not the Same as Being a Friend

"Education is not about controlling a child;
it is about preparing them for life."
— Içami Tiba

Many mothers deeply love their children.
They care for them, listen to them, and make an effort every day to do everything right.
However, in the midst of so many voices, pieces of advice, and new parenting approaches, many have begun to feel confused, exhausted, and constantly afraid of making mistakes.
Each day becomes a new challenge, not only as parents, but also socially and within the family.
The moment you share the news that you are pregnant, opinions begin to arrive.
Well-intentioned advice, inherited recommendations, phrases repeated over and over again.
Many come from a place of love, yet among them they are often contradictory.
"You have to be your children's friend," they told me.
My heart beat faster.
I wondered where that idea had come from.
I had always heard that there is only one mother.
Friends they would have many throughout their lives, but that unique place of being their mother belonged only to me.
Even so, deep inside, I was consumed by the fear of being wrong, of not doing things correctly, of not being for my children everything I had set out to be.
That was when the questions began:
What does responsible parenting really consist of?
Where does love end and authority begin?
Is it possible to raise children with tenderness without giving up the role of guide?

To understand how we arrived here, it is necessary to look back for a moment.

For many years—from the nineteenth century well into the twentieth century—education in Europe and Latin America was shaped by a model of traditional authoritarianism, based on blind obedience.

The child was seen as a "small adult" who was expected to work, serve, and obey without questioning.

"The letter enters with blood" was a common phrase, widely accepted and normalized.

I remember listening to my grandfather tell his story.

He was the oldest of eight siblings and, after his father's death, at barely fourteen years old, he left school to help his mother.

He did not only abandon his studies; he also left behind his dream of becoming an architect.

He eventually worked in the carpentry workshop that had belonged to his father, while one of his brothers was able to continue studying.

At that time, leaving school in order to work was common.

Education was rigid, hierarchical, and unidirectional.

At home and at school, authority was imposed without dialogue; the adult was the owner of knowledge, and the child assumed a passive role, with little space for creativity, critical thinking, or autonomy.

Discipline was sustained through fear, punishment, and threat.

The child learned to obey through submission, not through understanding or responsibility.
Today, many older adults remember those stages through stories that reveal deep wounds: low self-esteem, normalized violence, fear of making mistakes, and an obedience that replaced the development of independent thought.
Parenting has also changed over time.
The way we educate our children does not arise out of nowhere.
It is the result of social, cultural, and emotional contexts that have been transforming from generation to generation.
Between the 1950s and 1970s, across much of the United States and the Western Christian world, a normative and religious approach to parenting predominated, centered on duty, rigid morality, and fear of punishment—whether divine or social.
Family roles were clearly defined, and obedience was considered an unquestionable virtue.
Later, during the 1980s and 1990s, with the massive incorporation of both parents into the labor market—especially in urban contexts and developed countries—what Brazilian psychiatrist Içami Tiba called substitution parenting began to emerge.
Shared time gradually began to be replaced by objects, gifts, and constant stimulation.
This gave rise to the concept of the "object child"—a child who is offered much, but from whom little is required.
With the arrival of the new millennium, particularly between the years 2000 and 2015, what became known as helicopter parenting gained strength.

Parents who were present, attentive, and well-intentioned, yet excessively protective.
Adults who constantly hover over their children's lives to prevent any frustration, mistake, or pain, believing that in doing so they are protecting them.
And in recent years, driven by social media, books, and digital movements, conscious parenting—also known as "lighthouse parenting"—has emerged.
A proposal that seeks to emotionally connect with the child, validate their feelings, and support their autonomy.

Raising children with awareness is the intentional exercise of authority through the strength of love, presence, and responsibility.

Here emerges the figure of the "subject child": a child recognized as an individual, with their own voice and emotions.
This latest approach is born from a deeply valuable intention: not to repeat the mistakes of the past.
However, in many households, the pursuit of connection has been accompanied by a loss of clarity in the adult role.
Thus, without realizing it, we moved from rigid models to diffuse ones.
From excessive control to fear of setting limits, from forced obedience to constant negotiation.
Along this journey, two voices stand out as especially clear in helping us understand what

many families are experiencing today.

Developmental psychologist Diana Baumrind was one of the first to systematically study parenting styles.

Through her research, she identified that not all educational models produce the same effects on children.

Baumrind described three major parenting styles—which were later expanded—but one stood out above the rest: the authoritative style.

This model combines affection, communication, and clear boundaries.

Neither extreme harshness nor permissiveness without direction.

According to her studies, children who grow up in environments where there is love, along with firm and consistent rules, develop greater emotional security, better self-regulation, and a stronger sense of responsibility.

A child's strength grows through the steady presence of adults who guide with clarity and purpose.

From Latin America, Brazilian psychiatrist Içami Tiba observed a similar phenomenon through his clinical practice.

For him, one of the greatest mistakes of modern parenting was the confusion of roles within the family.

Tiba insisted that parents are not friends.

They are references, role models, and those responsible for preparing their children for life in society.

When adults give up that place out of fear of frustrating or upsetting their children, the child is left without structure.
He was the one who spoke of the "object child": a child who is offered everything, but from whom little is required.
A child surrounded by stimulation, yet lacking limits.
He warned that this form of parenting creates a foundation of insecurity in a child.
Both Baumrind and Tiba, from different contexts, agree on something fundamental:
children need love, but they also need direction.
They need to be heard, but not burdened with decisions they are not yet able to carry.
After so many models, theories, and approaches, the question remains the same:
what do our children truly need?
Psychology and lived experience agree on something simple, though not always easy:
children need adults who love them deeply, but who do not give up guiding them.
Well-exercised authority is the guardian of childhood; it provides the structure and direction that keep it safe.

Scripture expresses this with serene clarity:

*"Start children off on the way they should go,
and even when they are old they will not turn from it."*
— Proverbs 22:6 (NIV)

Raising children with love and firmness is the responsible embrace of the sacred role entrusted to us.

In Hanna's Universe

"Love Sets Boundaries"

Hanna was sitting on the living room floor, surrounded by colorful pieces.
 She had taken all the toys out of the basket and was now trying to build something that existed only in her imagination.
"Just five more minutes," she said without looking up.
Her mother watched her in silence.
 She knew that scene well.
 She knew that if she didn't intervene now, those five minutes would turn into twenty, and then into exhaustion, frustration, and a difficult night.
"Hanna," she said softly, "it's time to put things away."
Hanna frowned.
 She squeezed a piece tightly in her hands and shook her head.
"But I'm not finished yet."
Her mother knelt beside her.
 She didn't raise her voice.
 She didn't overexplain.
"I understand that you want to keep going," she replied.
 "And even so, it's time to clean up."
Hanna let out a heavy sigh.
 Her eyes filled with anger and sadness at the same time.

For a moment, her mother felt the impulse to give in.
 To let it slide.
 To avoid the tears.
But she didn't.
She stayed there—present.
 Steady.
 Close.
"I'll help you," she added, "but we are going to put things away."
Hanna was not happy.
 She put the pieces away slowly, dragging her feet.
It was not a perfect scene.
And yet, when the last toy returned to the basket, something shifted.
 Hanna's body relaxed.
 Her frown softened.
 The living room grew calm.
Later that night, before going to sleep, Hanna curled up next to her mother.
"Thank you for helping me," she whispered.
Her mother held her close.
 She had not been her friend in that moment.
 She had been her guide.

Love is the steady presence that protects a child's heart.

Chapter 2

The child's brain needs structure

For a child to feel safe and develop an integrated brain,
 they need the structure of clear limits combined with the warmth of deep connection.
 — Adapted from The Whole-Brain Child
 — Daniel J. Siegel

While I was living in Brazil, I met a woman who was deeply loving and fiercely protective of her son. We will call this little boy Mateo.

Mateo became my youngest son's best friend. They were in K-4 (preschool), and my son would often come home with stories about him. Many times, he would say that Mateo did not want to play because, in his words, "everything scared him."

My son could not understand it. He would ask me why Mateo was afraid to go down the slide, to ask for a second serving of beans, or to play soccer.

One day, we went to their house, and something immediately caught our attention.

The house was completely covered with protective netting. It almost looked like a prison.

It was a beautiful two-story home, yet there was not a single window without mesh. His mother had even chosen a house without a swimming pool, fearing that Mateo might jump into the water without her noticing.

Seeing this was unsettling.

In contrast, my decision had been to teach my little one how to swim and, if he fell, to help him get back up.

And yet, I felt like a bad mother for not offering him more protection.

Then the question arose:

What is the right way?

Over the years — and after a few stumbles of my own — I have discovered that there is no single correct way to raise a child.

However, there are principles we must understand in order to bring balance to our role as parents.

Our children need security, but they also need space to develop independence.
They need to feel supported without feeling confined.

Finding that balance is not always easy.
Before mentioning some of the psychologists and psychiatrists who help us understand this process, I want to pause and reflect on a truth that places all of us in the same position of learning — a truth rooted in wisdom.

The Bible expresses it this way:

"Therefore everyone who hears these words of Mine and puts them into practice
is like a wise man
who built his house on the rock."
— Matthew 7:24

Structure — formed by boundaries and values — is the rock that keeps a child from collapsing when the storms of life arrive.
This is where this chapter truly begins: with the need to define boundaries and values that provide structure for both the brain and the heart of our children.
We need only remember those geography lessons in which we learned to identify borders. We knew precisely where one country ended and another began.
One definition that stayed with me from that time is this:
A boundary is the point where my freedom ends and another person's freedom begins.

Such a simple definition, and yet so profound.

Values, on the other hand, can be understood as an inner compass — one that guides us in choosing which path to take, allowing us to move forward without harming others and creating spaces where everyone can feel safe.

Structure in childhood is like a map.

A map that keeps a child's brain from getting lost in chaos.

When we bring order to their days — through habits, routines, and small repeated moments — we are helping to shape a brain that can remain calm even when storms come.

When a child does not know what will happen next, the defense system activates again and again, searching for danger even where there is none. The body shifts into survival mode.

In contrast, when a child knows what comes next — for example, that drawing time follows the devotional — the nervous system can relax.

The brain no longer needs to defend itself and can move from a state of alertness to a state of learning.

Siegel explains that a brain capable of anticipating the immediate future is a brain that feels safe.

That sense of safety is the foundation upon which self-regulation is gradually built.

But there is something even more important: Structure only works when it is accompanied by emotional connection.

Siegel summarizes this in a simple idea: connect before you redirect.

When there are rules without relationship, the brain drifts toward rigidity.

When there is love without structure, it drifts into chaos.

Integration occurs when a child feels supported and guided at the same time.

From this perspective, structure offers the child what Siegel calls the four S's: feeling safe, seen, soothed, and secure.

Confidence grows from that place — not from fear. Educating our children is, perhaps, the greatest challenge of our lives.

Each day we strive to become better parents, observing ourselves and often comparing ourselves — sometimes without realizing it — to the families around us.

In every home we see different styles, different outcomes, different paths.

In the midst of that diversity, we often become our own harshest critics.

As we explored earlier when examining the work of Diana Baumrind, her research was not only theoretical but deeply practical. Although her theory initially centered on three fundamental parenting styles, over time — and through the follow-up of more than one hundred families from preschool through adolescence — her model expanded to more precisely identify how different approaches to parenting leave visible marks on children's emotional and behavioral development.

To better understand this influence, we will now look more closely at the four major parenting styles that complete her research. Keeping in mind the authoritative style — the one that seeks balance between warmth and clear limits — we can contrast it with the other models to understand why some prove more effective than others.

- **The authoritarian style**: Rules are imposed without dialogue, and obedience is demanded through fear or punishment. In these homes, children often learn to follow rules, but they struggle to make decisions, manage frustration, and trust themselves.
- **The permissive style**: Parents are loving and communicative but provide few clear limits. Although these children often feel heard, the lack of structure can lead to impulsivity, immaturity, and difficulty with self-regulation.
- **The authoritative** (or democratic) style: Considered the most balanced. Here, parents combine warmth with firm boundaries. They listen to their children and explain expectations, yet they do not relinquish their role as guides. Children raised in this environment tend to develop stronger self-esteem, responsibility, and confidence.
- **The neglectful style**: This fourth style, which completes the research, is characterized by emotional absence. Parents meet basic needs but remain largely uninvolved. This type of upbringing leaves deep wounds, as the child grows up without feeling seen, accompanied, or supported.

As we learn about these styles, it is natural to ask:
Which one do I recognize in myself?
Most of us do not fit perfectly into just one.
We tend to move between them, depending on our level of exhaustion, the season of life, or the

situation.

Understanding them gives us something valuable: awareness.

Awareness to choose more intentionally how we want to guide our children.

Parenting with structure requires confidence in the decisions we make.

Many times, we parent with doubt, with exhaustion, and with fear of making mistakes.

Even so, setting limits remains an act of care.

Because we understand that our children need more than affection — they need guidance.

Children thrive with present adults who hold the boundary and walk alongside them through the emotions that follow.

Structure provides the necessary framework for a child to face and navigate discomfort with courage.

As we accompany this process — embracing every mistake, lesson, and adjustment — we grow in wisdom and maturity as parents as well.

In Hanna's Universe

"Love Sets Boundaries"

Hanna was sitting on the living room floor,
surrounded by colorful building pieces.
She had taken all the toys out of the basket and
was now trying to build something that existed
only in her imagination.
"Just five more minutes," she said without
looking up.
Her mother watched her in silence.
She knew that scene well. She had learned to
recognize what usually came next.
If she did not step in now, those five minutes
would turn into twenty, and then into exhaustion,
frustration, and a difficult night.
"Hanna," she said gently, "it's time to clean up."
Hanna frowned.
She squeezed a piece tightly in her hands and
shook her head.
"But I'm not finished yet."
Her mother knelt beside her.
She did not raise her voice.
She did not offer a long explanation.
"I understand that you want to keep going," she
replied.
 "And it is still time to clean up."
Hanna sighed deeply.
Her eyes filled with anger and sadness at the
same time. For a brief moment, her mother felt

the impulse to give in, to let it go, to avoid the tears.

But she did not.

She stayed there. Present. Firm. Close.

"I'll help you," she added, "but we're going to put the toys away."

Hanna was not happy.

She put the pieces away slowly, dragging her feet.

It was not a perfect moment.

And yet, when the last toy returned to the basket, something shifted.

Hanna's body relaxed.

Her brow softened.

The room grew calm.

Later that night, before going to sleep, Hanna curled up next to her mother.

"Thank you for helping me," she whispered.

Her mother held her close.

In that moment, she was not trying to be her friend.

She was being her guide.

Love does not always look like agreement.

Sometimes, it looks like holding the boundary with calm and staying close through the discomfort.

Structure is the steady support that sustains our children's development.

Chapter 3

When Boundaries Stir Emotions

"A limit does not fail because there is crying; crying is the process through which the child accepts reality."
— Rudolf Dreikurs, Children: The Challenge (1964)

Confronting My Own Paradigms

For a long time, I believed that noise, disorder, and chaos were an inevitable part of childhood.

Because I have lived in different countries, I had the opportunity to observe how children are raised and educated in very different cultural contexts. Those experiences confronted me more than once.

In Brazil, for example, I was struck by the calm atmosphere of the school my children attended. I would walk into the classrooms and it almost seemed as if there were no classes taking place. The environment was peaceful, the children moved freely, and yet there was order.

I came from Colombia, where I had worked as a mathematics and physics teacher, accustomed to long days, constant noise, and exhaustion at the end of each day. Seeing that contrast made me wonder: how had they achieved that balance without shouting or constant tension?

At the same time, I also had to confront my own reactions as a mother.

If a child did not obey, the reprimand was strong. I do not say this with pride, but with honesty.

Later, while living in Canada, I visited a young family whose children were a few years younger than mine. As I spoke with the mother — practicing my English — her daughter began running around the table. On the table there was a glass of water and, next to it, a computer.

I watched the scene nervously. In my world, serving a small child water in a glass cup was unthinkable.

The mother warned her several times to be careful.

The child did not listen, and what was expected, happened: the glass fell, the water spilled, and the girl looked at her mother in fear.
Almost automatically, I prepared myself for crying, shouting, and fear.
But that did not happen.
The mother approached calmly and said, "Hey, don't move. It was an accident."
She cleaned up the mess and protected her daughter from getting hurt by the broken glass.
That scene stayed with me.
To this day, those two episodes — Brazil and Canada — continue to return to my mind.
Not to decide who was right, but to ask myself a more honest question:
What do we as adults do in the face of a child's emotion?

The real challenge: holding the limit.
Setting a boundary is usually not the hardest part of parenting.
What is truly challenging is holding that boundary when it provokes tears, anger, or frustration.
Seeing our children cry activates something in us. We want to help, to calm, to fix.
Sometimes we even want to prevent them from feeling that discomfort at any cost.
It is often said that to deprive a child of frustration is to deprive them of the development of resilience.
But then the inevitable question arises: how much frustration is acceptable? Where is the line between guiding and allowing too much?

I do not intend to answer these questions in absolute terms.

But if, as a parent, you have asked yourself these same questions, it may comfort you to know that you are not alone.

Rudolf Dreikurs, an Austrian psychiatrist and educator, took a deep interest in children's behavior from an angle that had not been widely explored at the time.

For him, children seek something essential: to feel significant and valued within the family.

When a child is unable to meet that need in positive ways, they may turn to challenging behaviors. Dreikurs identified some of these patterns, such as excessive attention-seeking, power struggles, revenge, or what he called assumed inadequacy — a state in which the child becomes so convinced that they cannot succeed that they stop trying altogether.

These behaviors do not appear out of nowhere. They are attempts — misguided, yet understandable — to belong.

And here is a difficult truth to accept: many times, in trying to avoid tears or conflict, we end up reinforcing precisely what we are trying to correct.

Dreikurs was clear about one thing: **we cannot protect our children from life; therefore, we must prepare them for it.**

When we feel excessive pity in the face of our children's frustration, we run the risk of rescuing them again and again. And in doing so, without realizing it, we weaken their ability to face reality.

We must accompany without canceling.
Boundaries, Participation, and Consequences
Dreikurs also observed that when children
participate — in ways appropriate to their age — in
family life, they tend to become more cooperative
and secure.

When they are able to help, express their opinions,
and understand the rules, they are more likely to
respect them not out of fear, but out of a sense of
belonging.

Instead of arbitrary punishments, he proposed
working with consequences.

Natural consequences are what happen without
adult intervention (if you do not eat, you will be
hungry).

Logical consequences are agreed upon beforehand
and directly related to the behavior (if you spill the
milk, you help clean it up).

Consequences teach responsibility within a
framework of respect.

Real love focuses, with tenderness, on long-term
well-being. It gives the child the opportunity to
move through their own discomfort as a sign of
deep confidence in their capacity to grow.

Up to this point, we have recognized discipline as a
profound act of love.

By contemplating the true essence of love, we
discover a truth that guides our steps and provides
us with unwavering security.

"Because the Lord disciplines the one He loves,
as a father disciplines the son he delights in."
— Proverbs 3:12

 In this verse, God reveals His heart as Father.
He does not present discipline as punishment, but
as an expression of love.
He assumes something important: the one who
loves, disciplines.
Many of us have cried at some point in life and,
over time, have come to recognize God even
through that process.
Discomfort did not cancel love; it revealed it.
In the same way, when we understand discipline as
an act of love, we can guide our children with
greater clarity and less guilt.
Leading them along the right path means preparing
them to walk with firmness. And this is where the
promise appears: when they are guided with love
and truth, even as they grow older, they will carry
that path in their hearts.
Accompanying our children's frustration is a deep
process that allows us to connect with our own
emotions, with our personal history, and with our
natural desire to protect their well-being.
Crying, becoming angry, or resisting indicates that a
child is facing a reality they are still learning to
manage. Our role is to remain present while that
process unfolds.
Holding the boundary while accompanying the
tears is a form of love that embraces future well-
being and looks beyond the immediate moment
with hope.

Education is about walking with our children as they learn to move through each discomfort. And along that path — with mistakes, doubts, and learning — we grow as well, learning to love with firmness and to guide with responsibility.

In Hanna's Universe

"When Understanding Changes the Way We See"

Hanna was sitting on the floor, feeding her doll.
 She had placed it carefully, as if it were a real baby.
Sagu, her adorable rabbit, pretended to be the
father.
 Dogui, always cheerful, played the role of the older
brother.
 Michiko, her serious cat, had been given the most
uncomfortable role: the younger sibling.
Hanna was not imitating anyone in particular;
 she was simply playing at caring, the way children
do when they are trying to understand the world.
Her mother watched from a short distance.
For a moment, the game flowed without any
problems.
 Until Hanna suddenly stopped.
She set the doll aside, crossed her arms, and
frowned. —This baby won't stop crying —she said,
annoyed—.
 I'm tired of it.
 The game is over for today.
Sagu lifted his ears.
 Dogui gave a small jump.
 Michiko remained still.
The three of them moved closer to Mom, as if
looking for shelter.
She approached slowly and sat down in front of
Hanna. At first, she didn't say anything.
—Hanna —she finally asked—, why do you think
this baby is crying so much?

Hanna didn't answer right away.
She looked at the doll.
 Then she looked at Michiko, who remained serious
in his role as the younger sibling.
—I don't know... —she murmured—.
 Maybe she's hungry.
 Or tired.
 Or she doesn't know how to say what she wants.
Her mother nodded.
—And what do you think she needs when she cries
like that?
Hanna sighed.
—Someone to hold her...
 or to help her...
 or to not leave her alone.
The doll was still on the floor.
Hanna looked at it a little longer this time.
 She didn't seem less upset,
 but something had changed.
She slowly uncrossed her arms, picked up the doll,
and held it carefully.
—Okay —she said—.
 I'll keep playing...
 but I need help.
Her mother smiled.
 She didn't solve the game.
 She didn't give instructions.
She simply stayed close, watching.
And Hanna kept playing,
 not because the crying had disappeared,
 but because she had begun to understand it.

Do not do for your child what they can learn to do for themselves;
every time you do, you take away their opportunity to discover their own strength.

Chapter 4

Children Need Consistent Adults

"Trust in the attachment figure is the foundation upon which a stable and secure personality is built."

— John Bowlby, A Secure Base (1988)

Children Need Predictable Adults

Talking about being present in our children's lives inevitably leads us to reflect on the reality of families today.
 We live in a time where many different family contexts exist: single-parent households, absent parents, children raised by grandparents, or cared for by nannies who genuinely participate in their emotional upbringing.
This topic could easily be expanded much further and would deserve an entire book of its own.
 For now, I want to return to the center: the child.
Regardless of circumstances, every child needs parents—or at least one responsible adult—who remains consistently present in their life and lovingly assumes the task of raising and guiding them during their early years.
One question that naturally arises is that of attachment.
As human beings, we form attachments to the people around us who influence our lives. In childhood, this bond is not optional; it is vital.
 Children, especially during the period of breastfeeding, develop a deep attachment to their mother.
I remember being told many times:
 — Don't hold the baby so much, you'll spoil them.
At that time, even though breastfeeding was a painful and demanding process, after nine months the attachment I felt toward that little creature—perfect in my eyes—was immense.
 And that experience led me to ask myself:

how can something so natural and necessary be
seen as harmful?

Attachment or Dependence?

John Bowlby, a British psychiatrist and
psychoanalyst, developed attachment theory and
profoundly transformed our understanding of
human relationships and emotional development.
Over the years, as I have met people from different
cultures, I have noticed that regardless of the
country, some individuals find it easier to build
healthy relationships—with family or friends—
while others experience more unstable, selective, or
even conflictive bonds. Many times, these patterns
were also reflected in their children and in the way
they related to mine.
Bowlby's work is grounded in a central idea:
children are born with a biological system
programmed to seek closeness to a caregiver.
 Not only for food, but for emotional survival.
When a child knows that their attachment figure is
available and responds sensitively to their needs,
they feel safe.
 And it is precisely this sense of safety that gives
them the courage to explore the world.
Here we encounter what Bowlby called the
attachment paradox:
 the more secure and "attached" a child feels to their
parents, the more independent and autonomous
they become.
This connects deeply with the idea of preparing a
child for life, not holding them back.

Sometimes we mistakenly believe that attachment and limits are opposing concepts.

But they are not.

Without connection, limits feel like aggression.

Without limits, attachment turns into overprotection that weakens the child.

Bowlby described the mother as a secure harbor to which the child can return to refuel, but also as the launching ramp that encourages them to go back out into the world.

Poor parenting does not occur when a child faces difficulties, but when the adult tries to prevent all suffering by removing every obstacle from their path.

Secure attachment, on the other hand, is built when the adult accompanies the child as they face the obstacle, offering the comfort needed so they do not give up.

Attending to a child's emotion is not the same as negotiating the limit.

If a child cries because there are no sweets, a mother with secure attachment can hold them and say:

— I understand that you're sad. It hurts me to see you suffer. But the rule still stands.

Here, there is emotional presence and also consistency.

There is attachment, and there is discipline. Responding to a child's stress is not rewarding misbehavior.

It is helping regulate their nervous system so that, once calm, learning can take place.

Learning happens in a state of safety; a calm heart

is the essential foundation for growth and understanding.

For a long time, I felt confronted by the idea that as a mother I needed to be available twenty-four hours a day, often even to meet my children's whims.

This exhausted me physically and emotionally, because that kind of constant availability is nearly impossible—even when living under the same roof.

I had the privilege of raising my children alongside my husband, who lovingly gave me space to rest, especially during the months of breastfeeding.

I know that this is not the reality for all mothers, and today I can better understand the frustration and exhaustion that many experience.

That exhaustion often led me, without realizing it, to inconsistency when setting limits.

Over time, I came to understand something essential: a consistent mother is predictable.

The child knows that if they are afraid, she will respond with empathy.

And the firm mother—as Dreikurs would say—is respectful: the child knows that if a rule is broken, there will be a logical consequence.

The greatest lack of attachment is not firmness.

It is inconsistency.

Consistency is, in fact, one of the purest acts of love, because it frees the child from the burden of having to guess what kind of mother they will encounter today.

I do not want to close this chapter without returning to the most important guiding voice.

"The Lord is good;
his love endures forever;
his faithfulness continues through all generations."
— Psalm 100:5

Just as God's faithfulness is an unwavering anchor for us, our consistency in parenting is a steady gift that remains firm regardless of a child's mood. Consistency is the practice of grace; it is the daily reflection of God's eternal faithfulness in the heart of our homes.

In Hanna's Universe

"When Being Close Can Be Felt."

Hanna was sitting on the edge of her bed, talking
with Dogui and Sagu.
 Dogui listened attentively.
 Sagu, her sweet little rabbit, nodded as if every
story truly mattered.
Michiko was a bit farther away, watching them.
Hanna paused and smiled.
—You were in this story too! —she said happily,
looking at Michiko.
Michiko lifted his head, walked over, and gave a
small hop to her side, purring.
Hanna gently stroked him.
—I like it better this way —she said—
 when we're all together.
Sagu spoke softly:
—This group isn't complete if one is missing.
Everyone laughed.
Michiko settled close to Hanna and said:
—I'm always watching you, Hanna.
 Even if you don't always see me, I'm close.
 And when you need me, you know I'm here.
Hanna looked around at her friends and felt steady
again.
 She didn't need to say anything else.

*Secure attachment is built when the adult is predictable,
accessible, and emotionally available.*

Chapter 5

Education Is the Formation of Habits

"Predictability helps the child's brain feel safe and organize emotions."

— Daniel J. Siegel, The Whole-Brain Child (2012

Forming Habits: A Path Toward Emotional Order
Forming habits is a profound learning process for us as adults. Sustaining them requires living each routine as an act of care and an opportunity for growth, beyond the sense of burden that sometimes appears in daily life. We long to see organization, responsibility, and consistency in our children, and that desire pushes us to cultivate those same virtues in our own lives.

And then an uncomfortable but honest question arises:

How do we expect to form habits in our children if we have not first integrated them ourselves?

It is not simple. But it is necessary, and it begins with our intention.

We live in a world where difficulty is resolved with a click, where waiting feels uncomfortable and immediacy has become the norm.

In the midst of that reality, forming habits in our children is a vital necessity and a call to intentionality.

And with that urgency come the questions:

At what age are habits formed? Is it already too late? Which habits will truly serve them for life?

Before answering these questions, I want to pause on a principle that is as simple as it is foundational.

I still remember how, in my childhood, my mother sent us to bed at 9:30 p.m. That hour marked the conclusion of the family television block, signaling the natural time for our rest. I do not know how parents managed before that, but what I do know is that the clarity of that boundary gave us direction.

Bedtime has always been one of the most

challenging moments in parenting.

 Many children are not accustomed to a consistent schedule. During the week, school helps maintain order; on weekends, everything tends to fall apart. That is why, in my time, that habit was so valuable —even supported by something as ordinary as television.

Just as in the 1980s the music of the evening news signaled, without words, that our time had ended and it was time for bed, today our routines must serve the same purpose.

They must be the music that quiets the noise of the world and awakens emotional order in the hearts of our children.

As parents, we are aware of the importance of creating routines to provide structure and peace. Emotional order is born from predictability. When a child knows what to expect from their mother, their nervous system organizes itself. For a young child, the world is a place of constant discovery, where the guidance of an adult gives meaning, belonging, and order.

Predictability allows them to feel safe and to experience a minimal sense of control over their own lives.

From a neuroscientific perspective—as Daniel J. Siegel explains—when a child knows what comes next, the amygdala, the center of fear and alertness, can relax.

When the day is unpredictable, the child lives in a state of red alert. The body produces cortisol, and in that state, the child cannot cooperate or learn; they can only fight or flee, which often appears as

tantrums.
When the day is predictable, the brain enters an energy-saving mode.
The energy that is not spent trying to guess what will happen next is used to learn, create, and connect.
Many parents believe that being predictable means being boring or rigid.
Içami Tiba would say the opposite: a child without predictable routines is a child enslaved by impulses and by the mood of the adults around them; a child with clear habits is a free child, because they understand how their world works and can move within it with greater confidence.
Today we know that forming habits not only creates mental structure, but also builds autonomy and emotional security.
Predictability is not built only through schedules; it is built, above all, through communication.
From the moment a child is born, a mother begins communicating long before words appear. She learns to read the cry, the gesture, the posture, the silence. Without manuals or instructions—often instinctively—she responds to those needs.
That early communication—verbal and nonverbal—is the foundation of attachment and is built through daily presence. The great challenge of motherhood appears when the child grows and communication requires order, coherence, and consistency. What was once intuitive must become intentional.
When we speak of forming habits, communication plays a fundamental role.

A child sustains a routine more easily when they clearly understand what is expected of them. Effective communication means saying what is necessary, with clarity and consistency.

Anticipating the steps of the day is a profound act of care. Simple phrases such as "after dinner, we take a bath, and then it's time for bed" organize the child's internal world and provide essential security. Clear communication reduces anxiety; when a child knows what comes next, their body relaxes and settles into a state of calm.

Often, our children are trying to orient themselves amid the messages they receive, so coherence in our words helps them find direction. To communicate is to establish a boundary with firmness and love. Validating emotion is an act of empathy that remains united with the established rule. When we say, "I understand that you are sad," the words accompany the feeling while the boundary sustains the necessary structure.

When words and actions align, the child learns to trust. Communication thus becomes an invisible habit that organizes, anticipates, and sustains daily life.

From Chaos to Habit Formation

We begin with something fundamental: communication will be one of our most important tools in this process.

Often, in the midst of daily chaos, we feel that we do not understand our children. We interpret their reactions as disobedience or bad character, when in

reality many of them reflect a lack of habits and an environment that is not predictable.
Understanding this changes our perspective.
Communication flows in harmony with the formation of habits, evolving as they take root. For that reason, I want to begin with a specific habit that holds profound power for the peace and rhythm of family life.

The Habit of Emotional Order

Order is not only about physical space.
An organized environment directly affects emotional and mental state.
Living in an organized space generates a sense of control and psychological well-being. The brain interprets that environment as predictable, which reduces mental overload.
On the contrary, constant disorder—the accumulation of objects and excess visual stimuli—can increase irritability, affect attention, and create a persistent sense of overwhelm.
This is especially important in childhood.
A child does not yet have the internal resources to filter external chaos; the environment fulfills that function for them.
For that reason, establishing simple routines of organization is not a whim or an aesthetic demand. It is a concrete way to help a child regulate themselves. And this is within reach of any home, regardless of size or resources.
I remember a woman who was emotionally overwhelmed. Her house was always disorganized,

filled with old and broken objects. She had a young child, and his behavior clearly reflected that environment.

The child was barely four years old and showed intense frustration. His mother felt overwhelmed and said she could not "control" him.

A simple idea emerged: organize a space just for him—a corner with his toys and a small area where he could sit to play or draw.

Some time later, I visited again.

The rest of the house was the same, but that corner was cared for.

The mother told me that since her son had that space, his attitude had changed: he was calmer and less reactive.

I do not know what happened afterward with that family, but I confirmed something important: Sometimes, a small visual rest is enough to begin organizing a child's internal world.

This idea is not new. In Japan, there is a simple philosophy known as the 5S method, which seeks to create environments that help people live with greater clarity, respect, and balance.

It is not about perfection or immaculate homes, but about spaces that do not overload the mind.

Before trying to organize the mind, we can begin by organizing the space:

- Keep only what is necessary.
- Give each object a clear place.
- Maintain basic cleanliness.
- Sustain simple routines.
- Be consistent.

Where Do I Begin Without Feeling Overwhelmed?

You do not need to change your entire home or all
your routines.
We move one step at a time. Great decisions are
sustained through small steps.

First Habit: Emotional and Environmental Order

Begin with one single space:
It may be a toy box, a shelf, a desk, or a drawer of
shirts.
(This will be the first place where the child
experiences order and predictability.)
Fewer objects mean greater calm. To avoid
overstimulation, work more with clarity than with
quantity.
Suggestion: rotate toys; store some and leave visible
only those that are being used.
A place for everything, and everything in its place.
This is not about aesthetics, but about repetition.
When a child knows where something belongs and
what happens next, anxiety decreases.
At the beginning, the adult sustains the habit.
You organize together, you remind, and you mark
the closing.
This process reinforces learning. The habit remains
firm even when tears appear. Resistance to change
is a natural response that children often express
through crying.
If there are tears: accompany them and do not
retreat. Be firm with love.
Every routine needs a beginning and an ending.

Songs, repeated phrases, or clear gestures help the brain understand that something starts and something ends.

To close this chapter, take these three certainties with you:

- Focus on what is essential.
- Embrace your process.
- Be consistent, not perfect.

At the end of the day, order is a gift we give ourselves in order to find serenity. Our pursuit of balance has a divine design:

"For God is not a God of disorder but of peace."
— 1 Corinthians 14:33

When we organize our environment and our emotions, we prepare the space for His peace to dwell within us without obstruction. Make your space a reflection of that promise.

In Hanna's Universe

"When Order Reigns"

Hanna had spent the entire afternoon playing with her friends in her room.
 Sagu, her faithful rabbit, had gently reminded her to take a moment to organize her blouses, but she was busy—she had turned the sheets into a camping tent.
Mom had passed by the room several times.
 She observed.
 She smiled.
Suddenly, familiar sounds began to drift in from the kitchen.
 Mom was humming the song she always sings when dinner is almost ready.
Hanna jumped to her feet.
 The agreement was clear: before dinner, the room needed to be back in order.
She began moving quickly, unsure of where to start.
 Dogui barked and ran around her, playing.
Hanna let out a small shout.
Everything fell silent.
From beneath the sheets, Michico jumped out.
 "You're in a hurry," he said. "You already know where everything goes."
"But... where do I start?" Hanna asked.
Sagu walked over to the sheets.
 "Let's fold the tent first," he said. "Then

everything will fall into place."
Hanna began to tidy up.
 This time, calmly.
When she finished, the room felt different.
 It could breathe again.
Then she heard Mom's voice from the kitchen:
"Hanna, dinner is ready."

Predictability is the foundation of security that sustains our children's growth.

Chapter 6

Consistency and Integrity in the Adult

"A child's confidence is built when the adult remains consistently available."

— John Bowlby, A Secure Base (1988)

The integration of habits into family life reaches its maturity in our ability to sustain them. An adult's consistency is the foundation of a child's emotional security; it is the conscious decision to preserve order and structure as a gift of stability for the home. When we persevere, routine is transformed into a predictable refuge, filled with care.

Holding onto an important decision when daily demands confront us requires presence. Understanding the path is only the first step; walking it day after day is the true act of love.

I still remember with affection learning my multiplication tables as a child. My grandmother walked beside me in that process, using small wooden cards. On them, she wrote the operations and drew groups to represent each multiplication. We spent many afternoons playing that way until the tables settled into my memory. She would move from one number to another, attentively observing my learning. What marked my life beyond the method itself was her constant presence.

Today, as a mathematics and physics teacher, I reaffirm this truth: loving, sustained consistency is what produces lasting results. Presence, repeated over time, is what transforms a resource into real learning.

For John Bowlby, habit formation is deeply connected to emotional security. For a child to integrate a habit or explore their environment, they need a Secure Base. When the adult is steady and predictable, the child lives in a state of calm. From that place of rest, the brain can devote its resources to learning routines. Through presence, the adult lends their own nervous system to help the child regulate.

When the child recognizes that permanence, they internalize the adult's structure. What begins as a shared habit gradually becomes an autonomous ability. Through consistent presence, the child builds a mental map in which the world feels understandable. In this way, habits are integrated as a natural part of an organized and secure life.

The Message of Inconsistency

When adult permanence weakens, the process of habituation is interrupted. Separation anxiety takes the place of learning, and the child prioritizes securing the adult's attention and presence. Disorganization, irritability, or resistance to simple routines such as eating or sleeping are signs of a bond that needs to be reordered through presence. Building a strong bond requires a disposition that is cultivated day after day. Being a reliable reference means recognizing that the child needs us to hold, first, what we hope to see reflected in them. Consistency is rooted in emotional responsibility: the decision to return to the original purpose, to restore limits, and to sustain routines even in the midst of exhaustion.

The child finds rest in the adult who remains available, who does not contradict what is essential, and who keeps the course steady. In that coherence, the child is able to relax and trust.

Shared Learning

Parenting is also a learning process for the adult. Just as the child learns to organize themselves, we learn how to teach, how to sustain attachment without losing our place, and how to set limits without withdrawing from the relationship. Habit-building is a two-way path: while the child learns what to do, the adult learns how to be.
When the adult allows themselves to learn alongside the child, routine becomes a shared space. Each child is a unique being who needs to be recognized in their individuality. Parenting invites us to revisit our own paradigms and to consciously choose how we show up. When we accept the human and evolving nature of this journey, parenting becomes a living, attainable, and deeply meaningful experience.
Scripture offers us a clear and liberating guide:

"Train up a child in the way he should go, and when he is old he will not depart from it."
— Proverbs 22:6

To train a child in their way is to walk with them, to observe and support their personal discovery. God calls us to recognize each child's identity by name, honoring their character and their timing. The path is formed through loving repetition and daily coherence. When we embrace our role with faithfulness, habits become well-traveled paths walked in companionship. As we guide the child, we ourselves are also formed in the art of sustaining our own path.

The Gift: The Thread of the Yarn
(The Five-Minute Rule)

Sustaining consistency and coherence at home requires a starting point—a small thread to pull when the yarn of daily life feels hopelessly tangled. At times, the greatest difficulty is not the task itself, but knowing where to begin unraveling the overwhelm.

The Five-Minute Rule is that first movement toward calm: anything that takes five minutes or less is best done in the moment.

I often tell my students that subjects do not become difficult because of their complexity, but because we allow tasks to accumulate. What is simple, when postponed, loses its lightness and begins to weigh on us.

The same happens in parenting. That glass left on the table or that shoe out of place is not a problem in itself, but when we encounter it later, it becomes a quiet reminder of what remains unresolved. Little by little, these details turn into mental load that drains our energy.

Relieving this load is an act of self-care. Completing a small action immediately—making the bed, tidying a basic space, or deciding on a pending task —is a daily victory. These small wins lift our spirits and send a signal to the body that it is possible to sustain the path. True efficiency is a steady, rhythmic flow; it is the realization that the peace at the end of the day is the beautiful result of the

simple decisions we make in the present.
When you move with that clarity in small things, your child observes, imitates, and learns. Order stops feeling like an imposition and becomes a natural rhythm, built in your presence. By pulling this five-minute thread, you allow the entire structure of your home to align with your purpose, offering both yourself and your family a space of lightness and well-being.

In the Universe of Hanna

"The Rhythm of Creation in Everyday Life"

It was a quiet Sunday afternoon.
 Hanna had gone to church and returned home with a reflection she did not want to keep only to herself.
She gathered her friends and sat them in a circle, as if she were the teacher. Dogui, her faithful dog, curled up close beside her, watching every gesture with careful attention, as if he sensed that something important was about to begin.
Michiko, the cat, let out a small yawn, making it clear that he needed action. Just then, with two quick hops, Sagu—the gentle little rabbit—arrived. He sat up straight, very serious, and asked with curiosity:
"Alright, Hanna... what are you going to teach us today?"
Hanna sighed. She smoothed her dress and cleared her throat, like someone about to give a great speech.
"Today they told us that God is a God of order," she said. "And that even being God, He did not do everything in one single day. He divided creation into six days."
Michiko lifted his head immediately.
"And on the seventh, He rested!" he said firmly.
Hanna smiled.
"Exactly."

Michiko frowned slightly and added:
"Sometimes I leave everything to do on the last day... and I end up exhausted. You have to do what needs to be done, when it's time to do it."
A small silence settled in the room.
Dogui rested his head on the floor, as if the idea had reached his heart as well.
 Sagu nodded slowly.
Hanna looked around, and then she noticed something: a book had been left out of place, resting beside the couch. It wasn't serious. No one had mentioned it. But it was there.
Without interrupting the conversation, Hanna stood up, picked up the book, and placed it back on the shelf. The gesture was simple. Quick. Natural.
She sat down again.

A well-established habit is reclaimed time; the freedom to live in the present without the weight of what remains undone.

Chapter 7

Errors, Repair, and Grace

"The repair of interactive ruptures is the most powerful process in a child's development; it teaches that negativity can be overcome and that relationships can be restored."

— Dr. Ed Tronick, 2007

Often, mothers carry a definition of error that weighs more than it should. We have grown up under the idea that making a mistake means breaking something beyond repair, or that one bad moment erases all previous effort. From that place, error is experienced as a constant threat—to the relationship, to the bond, to the child's development.

However, developmental science, pedagogy, and clinical experience invite us to view error from a far more human and functional perspective. In these pages, we are not searching for a single correct way to be a mother, because that kind of perfection does not exist. What we are seeking is a clarification of concepts—frameworks studied by professionals that help us understand how we function as adults and how our children experience life. These principles serve as illuminating maps, offering us a clear and reliable path for our journey.

When we understand that error is information— and not condemnation—guilt loses its power. Making a mistake is not stepping off the path; it is an opportunity to model the most important process in life: repair. The adult who acknowledges an error, adjusts her pace, and returns to the relationship plants deep resilience in the child's heart. Grace is precisely that safe space where we accept our humanity while continuing to grow.

I grew up in a dysfunctional home. I experienced adult mistakes from the moment I was born, and over time that journey became a process of genuine transformation. Arriving where I am today—with the certainty that my parents' mistakes did not define me, but they did shape me—has been a profound realization. Those errors became warnings of what I do not want to repeat, but also examples of love, repair, and forgiveness.

As a Christian, I learned that God's love is expressed through grace. I understood that I cannot offer my children anything less. I also came to see that my parents, in turn, were shaped by the mistakes of those before them. We are part of a long story, and through us, that story is being transformed into a legacy of grace.

The Beauty of the Golden Scar

In Japan, there is an ancient art called *Kintsugi*. When a valuable ceramic piece breaks, master artisans do not attempt to hide the cracks with invisible glue. Instead, they join the fragments with resin mixed with gold powder.

The result is a piece that proudly displays its golden scars. For them, the vase is not "ruined"; on the contrary, its history of fracture and repair has made it more beautiful and unique.

As mothers, we sometimes fear that our mistakes will leave permanent marks on our children, as if we were fragile glass vases that must remain intact at all costs. Yet true mastery in parenting does not lie in the absence of cracks, but in our ability to apply the "gold" of repair.

When we make mistakes—because we are tired, because we lost patience, or because the demands of work overwhelmed us—and we return to the child to apologize, to explain, or to embrace, we are

practicing emotional Kintsugi. That crack, sealed
with the gold of grace and humility, strengthens the
bond. The child learns something vital: love is
capable of restoring what has been broken.
We are not striving to be perfect museum pieces—
cold and untouchable. We seek to be real mothers
who, with every repair, teach their children that in
this home, humanity is always welcome.

The Modern Error: Interrupted Presence

Today we face a challenge previous generations did
not know: digital distraction. Often, the mistake is
less about what we do and more about what we fail
to do. It is the presence that becomes fragmented
by the phone screen.
When we replace looking at our child with looking
at a device, we send an unintentional message:
"What is happening in this virtual world is more
important than what you are trying to
communicate to me."
Dr. Ed Tronick, in his research on connection,
demonstrated that a lack of emotional response—
the still face we sometimes adopt when looking at a
screen—creates distress in a child.
I once heard a mother proudly say that her
newborn "already knew" when photos were being
taken. What that baby registered was not the device,
but the shift in presence: the face that tightened, the
attention that moved away, the bond interrupted in
moments that, when repeated, begin to form a
habit.
Our presence preserves our time and our sacred

capacity for immediate repair.

If we do not notice that the vase has cracked because we are looking elsewhere, we cannot apply the gold of grace.

This disconnection is weakening children's ability to regulate their own emotions, because they cannot find in us the mirror through which to understand themselves.

Full presence is what teaches self-regulation. Offering attentive and consistent response is a liberating act of truth that strengthens our children's hearts.

Repair here means putting the device away. Putting it away in order to restore eye contact. It means integrating technology as a tool that serves us, ensuring that the path between our heart and our children's hearts remains clear.

The Value of Repair: A Principle-Based Approach

"A healthy family is not one without crises, but one that has learned to manage them with the honesty of recognizing its own mistakes." — Dr. David Hormachea (2002)

For many mothers, the name Dr. James Dobson may not be immediately familiar, yet his work has been foundational in homes and educational spaces through Focus on the Family. As a psychologist and author, Dobson devoted his life to reflecting on parenting as a vital balance between love, authority, and relationship. His contribution has been essential in giving language to something foundational: parenting is, above all, about sustaining connection.

Dobson helped establish the foundations of what we now understand as intentional parenting, based on pillars that give structure to the heart of the home. He taught that behavior is always a bridge of communication; behind every challenge or mistake lies an opportunity for connection. His approach emphasized protecting the child's spirit, distinguishing necessary discipline from harm to identity. For him, true authority is cultivated on the ground of emotional security: when a child feels deeply loved, their heart becomes receptive to instruction.

From this framework, principles we now consider fundamental—such as prioritizing relationship, practicing repair, and maintaining adult consistency—took shape in the daily language of families. If Kintsugi offers us a poetic vision of error, this professional approach confirms that relationship is always the priority. Error, when it occurs within an environment of clear principles, does not weaken a mother's authority; rather, it humanizes and strengthens it.

One essential principle in this model is: "Discipline without a solid relationship leads to rebellion, but discipline wrapped in love and grace builds character."

By recognizing the laws that govern human behavior, we better understand our own nature. Just as a vase responds to physical laws that explain its fragility, our patience has limits and our reactions can fail.

Accepting our humanity is the first step toward

embracing the grace that sustains our daily work. From this understanding, timely reconciliation becomes our most valuable tool. Dr. Dobson emphasized that the "gold" of repair appears after conflict: it is the moment when the adult takes the initiative to restore affection, ensuring that the child knows their value remains intact despite the mistake.

It is not about ignoring what happened, but about using the structure of the home to close the circle: acknowledging the fault, restoring affection, and reaffirming the boundary with clarity and gentleness. Grace, in this place, is the presence of a mother strong enough to admit her humanity and conscious enough to guide her child back to the path.

That same strength that allows us to acknowledge our humanity leads us to another foundational pillar in family formation. In the voice of Dr. David Hormachea, repair is directly linked to honesty and adult responsibility.

A healthy family grows through its challenges, leaning on a foundation of truth and integrity to navigate every season of life.

From this perspective, repair ceases to be merely an emotional act and becomes an act of character. A mother's leadership is strengthened when she is able to name reality without pride or avoidance. When grace is joined to responsibility, the tangled thread begins to loosen: error stops being an abyss and becomes the ground where character is formed —both ours and our children's.

The Grace of Forgiveness

Forgiveness is a foundational pillar of repair—a beautiful disposition that unfolds gracefully over time. It is a journey experienced in layers, where each step brings us closer to a restored and strengthened heart.
Forgiveness is a bridge to our past, allowing us to honor our journey as daughters. To forgive is to embrace our history with truth while releasing the weight of what we can no longer change, leaving our hands free for the present.
 In my own story, learning to forgive my parents meant understanding them as fragile human beings, shaped by their own histories. This forgiveness brought clarity to my past and gave me the freedom to release the weight, leaving me light and ready to carry only what belongs to my own journey.
There is also a forgiveness that lives in the present: forgiveness as mothers. Forgiving ourselves when we fall short, when we react out of exhaustion, when we fail despite our desire to do better. This forgiveness is not permissiveness or excuse; it is the place from which we can return to the relationship without being trapped in guilt. A mother who forgives herself can repair. A mother who does not forgive herself becomes paralyzed.
And there is a forgiveness that becomes instruction —the forgiveness we model for our children. When a child sees an adult acknowledge a mistake, ask for forgiveness, and try again, they learn something no isolated correction can teach: relationships are not

broken forever, love can restore, and making a mistake is not the end of the road.

Alongside forgiveness emerges another quiet yet essential pillar: humility. Humility is recognizing our own fragility and accepting that we are in a process of learning where it is always possible to ask for help. It is also the humility of submitting ourselves to principles, to relationships, and to a path we walk together.

Humility strengthens a mother's authority and makes her trustworthy. Children flourish with authentic adults—those who have the courage to say, "I was wrong," "I am learning to do better," or "Let's try again." In that gesture, authority becomes human and turns into a bridge of connection. Forgiveness and humility transform error. And it is in that space—where fragility is acknowledged and grace is received—that repair flourishes and the bond finds again its place of peace.

The Refuge of Grace

After walking the path of learning and seeking repair, we arrive at the place from which all our capacity to restore flows: the very source of grace. As mothers, we remember that before being guides to our children, we are daughters sustained by an eternal love. When the thread becomes tangled and our strength falters, we live under a permanent invitation:

"Let us then approach the throne of grace with confidence, so that we may receive mercy and find grace to help us in our time of need." — Hebrews 4:16

This is our greatest life principle: timely help. God invites us to come with complete confidence. The same security we desire our children to feel when they come to us is the security God offers us at every moment.

At this throne dwells the mercy that repairs our cracks with the gold of His love, allowing us to return home with restored hearts and ready to continue building.

Pillars of Chapter 7: Errors, Repair, and Grace

Relationship as Priority: Relationship is the ground where instruction takes root; without connection, discipline loses its purpose.

Integrity in Crisis: Family health lies in the honest management of conflict, taking responsibility for naming reality.

Repair as Gold: Error is an opportunity to model growth. Repair humanizes us and strengthens a child's resilience.

Forgiveness in Layers: A disposition that frees us from the past, removes guilt in the present, and models restoration for the future.

Trustworthy Humility: Embracing our fragility as parents strengthens our leadership, creating a safe and trustworthy sanctuary for our children.

In Hanna's Universe

The Grace of Forgiveness

Hanna woke up without wanting to go to school. It was Wednesday, and she loved Wednesdays because she had physical education. But that morning something was not right.
When she sat up in bed, the world seemed to spin. Without saying a word, she lay back down.
Her mother walked down the hallway carrying a basket of laundry. Without looking into the room, she called out in a hurried voice:
"It's time to get out of bed."
Hanna did not answer.
Five minutes later, Mommy passed by again.
"Get up, Hanna. It's time for school."
Hanna remained silent and turned toward the wall. Her body was burning with fever, but she did not know how to explain what she felt.
After a while, Michiko approached and meowed firmly:
"Enough laziness. It's time to go to school."
Dogui, instead, curled up at her feet, as if saying without words: we can stay a little longer.
A few minutes later, Mommy returned. This time she stepped into the room.
"You have to go," she said with irritation. "Your P.E. uniform is ready."
But as she moved closer, something stopped her.

She saw Hanna's face—pale and flushed at the same time. She reached out and touched her. She felt the heat.
Concern rushed in all at once.
Hanna opened her eyes and, with a small smile, looked at her.
"Mommy... I'm not going to school today."
Sagu gave two little hops and settled on Mommy's lap. Gently, as if speaking for everyone, he said:
"Everything is going to be okay."

Repair sustains the bond.

Chapter 8

Hope
(No One Arrives Too Late)

"Behold, I am making all things new."

— Revelation 21:5

There is a quiet idea that sometimes tries to settle in a mother's heart: the feeling that time has moved faster than our actions. We begin to believe that boundaries, habits, or the restoration of the cracks belong to a past that has already slipped away. Mature hope, however, is measured by the direction of the heart. In parenting, as long as the bond is still breathing, it is always the right moment. Formation is a flow of living processes. A child's brain carries remarkable plasticity; their character is a landscape that is continually being shaped, and their heart remains, by design, open to new experiences of connection.

Structure takes root today. Repair becomes the foundation of this very afternoon. Intention is born in this very moment.

Grace reminds us that the present is the place where our formative capacity lives. We raise our children with a vision of what they can become. Hope is the decision to shape with intention, to regulate in the middle of the storm, and to sustain the bond with steady devotion.

I. Hope Shapes with Vision

"O Lord of Heaven's Armies, if you look upon my suffering and answer my prayer and give me a son, I will give him to the Lord for all the days of his life."
— 1 Samuel 1:11
To understand the depth of intentional motherhood, we must look at the figure of Hannah. Her life stands as one of the clearest testimonies of a hope that does not wait passively but prepares itself.

After years in the desert of infertility, Hannah received Samuel with a sharpened awareness: the time he would spend under her roof would be brief.

That awareness transformed her hope into a strategic vision. Hannah raised Samuel with the sacred purpose of sending him out. Here we find one of the highest definitions of maternal success: our work is revealed in the fullness with which our children are prepared to go.

We educate to give them the wings of autonomy. We raise them so that one day we can release them in peace.

Aware that Samuel would soon live in the temple—an environment filled with great challenges—Hannah acted with extraordinary intentionality. She devoted herself to cultivating secure attachment: a bond so strong and so full of grace that it gave the child the freedom to release his mother's hand and hold firmly to the hand of God.

She nurtured in him a healthy autonomy and an inner security so deep that it became his greatest armor.

In those few years, she cultivated what was essential: rhythms of prayer, habits of order, and a discipline wrapped in love. This preparation became the solid ground on which Samuel's capacity for discernment grew. Years later, when a voice called to him in the silence of the night, Samuel was able to respond because he had learned to listen within the safety of his home. His mother's steady guidance had prepared his heart to recognize the Truth.

As mothers, our hope is nourished by this vision of the future. We recognize that the present is the right moment to build an inner security in our children—a refuge that will accompany them in every season and every place. By establishing clear boundaries and encouraging consistency, we shape their inner compass with love, giving them the confidence they need to walk with assurance.

II. Hope Regulates in the Midst of Tension

"Please, my lord, give her the living child. Do not kill him."
— 1 Kings 3:26

The story places us in the court of King Solomon before a dilemma that seems to have no solution: two women claim the motherhood of the same baby. In order to reveal the truth, the king proposes a radical solution—to divide the child in two with a sword.

In that instant of sudden crisis, where a single moment determines destiny, the true essence of motherhood emerges. While one of the women accepts the division, the real mother responds from a place of absolute clarity.

In those few years, she cultivated what was essential: rhythms of prayer, habits of order, and a discipline wrapped in love. This preparation became the solid ground on which Samuel's capacity for discernment grew. Years later, when a voice called to him in the silence of the night, Samuel was able to respond because he had learned to listen within the safety of his home. His mother's steady guidance had prepared his heart to recognize the Truth.

As mothers, our hope is nourished by this vision of the future. We recognize that the present is the right moment to build an inner security in our children—a refuge that will accompany them in every season and every place. By establishing clear boundaries and encouraging consistency, we shape their inner compass with love, giving them the confidence they need to walk with assurance.

II. Hope Regulates in the Midst of Tension

"Please, my lord, give her the living child. Do not kill him."
— 1 Kings 3:26

The story places us in the court of King Solomon before a dilemma that seems to have no solution: two women claim the motherhood of the same baby. In order to reveal the truth, the king proposes a radical solution—to divide the child in two with a sword.

In that instant of sudden crisis, where a single moment determines destiny, the true essence of motherhood emerges. While one of the women accepts the division, the real mother responds from a place of absolute clarity.

Her love chooses the preservation of her child above any claim of possession. She is willing to surrender her longing to keep the child if it ensures his life. She places life above the need to be right.

This scene reveals that hope is the capacity to regulate emotion under extreme pressure. The mother acts from the higher purpose of protecting what is essential, maintaining an inner calm that sustains life even when the environment becomes chaotic. In that moment, her love transforms the impulse for control into a generous surrender that preserves the bond.

In everyday parenting, we face our own "Solomonic judgments"—moments of intense tension in which our reactions shape the emotional well-being of our children. Emotional authority is the strength that allows us to sustain connection with integrity, choosing the child's well-being above the impulse of the moment. Like that mother, we discover that love is the wisdom of prioritizing peace so that our child's heart remains safe.

Here, hope becomes our capacity to remain calm in the present. It is the necessary pause that allows us to act with maturity and intention. When we regulate our response, we teach our children a fundamental truth: difficulties can become opportunities to strengthen our bond and draw us closer together.

Mature hope understands that caring for our child's heart is the greatest achievement of our motherhood.

III. Hope Repairs and Reorganizes

The science of attachment confirms our hope by showing us that the bond is a living relationship, strengthened through each new experience we share.
It is deeply valuable to understand that children develop an inner sense of security when they feel that the world is a safe place and that they themselves are worthy of being loved. This certainty is nourished by our consistent presence and, above all, by our willingness to strengthen the bond with tenderness in everyday life.
Your child's emotional destiny has the capacity to flourish through your present intention.
We are still in time to enrich that inner map:
Where rigidity has lived, flexibility can begin to grow today.
Where distance has existed, closeness can be cultivated today.
Where chaos has reigned, structure can be established today.
Mature hope recognizes that the family story remains alive. When we form with intention, regulate our emotions, and practice constant repair, we positively reorganize that inner map within the child. We teach them that love is a faithful presence that always finds its way back.

IV. Hope Matures Through the Process

Speaking about hope is easy when we reflect on biblical stories or the foundations of psychology. Real hope, however, is tested in everyday life: in the fatigue at the end of the day, in moments of doubt, and in those days when we feel we did not do things well.

As a mother and educator, I have gone through seasons when the idea of "having arrived too late" tried to paralyze me. Moments when I thought a boundary should have been established earlier, that a conversation had been postponed too long, or that a mistake could have prevented an unnecessary wound. Yet time has taught me a liberating truth: formation is not canceled by a stumble.

Parenting is the place where today's consistency becomes tomorrow's security. As we accompany the growth of our children, our own lives gain new depth, allowing us to live each stage with a maturity that only love and dedication can give.

I have witnessed how an intentional change in the way we communicate, greater consistency in our boundaries, or a renewed commitment to the bond can transform the atmosphere of a home. This transformation is not an instant event but an organic process.

If there is something I have confirmed along this journey, it is that children possess an admirable capacity to adapt.

They are deeply sensitive to change when it is born from an inner conviction within the adult.

When we bring order to our own inner world, the

family environment begins, almost by resonance, to reorganize itself.
 We are still in time to begin forming with intention.
Hope gives us the strength to inhabit every stage of the process. It is precisely in this steady journey that our maturity as mothers begins to flourish, becoming increasingly beautiful and resilient.

V. Hope Produces Excellent Wine

"Everyone brings out the choice wine first... but you have kept the best wine until now."
 — John 2:10

The miracle at the wedding in Cana offers clear insights for our work in the home. In this story, hope appears as an active disposition that prepares the setting for God to act.
Everything begins with quiet obedience: the water was always there, but the miracle required someone to fill the jars to the brim. In parenting, this translates into our daily consistency, into those habits and rhythms of love that may seem simple but become the raw material for a greater transformation.
This transformation unfolds under a clear maternal direction.
Mary, with the wisdom of one who knows where to turn, directs the need to the One who has the power to resolve it, reminding us that our task is to guide the hearts of our children toward the Source that can truly satisfy them. Jesus, in obedience to the

Father, elevates our daily offering—our water—into something new.

This miracle, though it takes place in the quietness of the jars, reveals itself as a blessing for an entire community. It reminds us that we do not raise our children only for the life of the home, but that we prepare them to become the "excellent wine" the world needs to receive. By strengthening our home, we are offering a gift to the generations to come. Your individual effort carries a reach that extends far beyond the present.

Often we believe that the best seasons have already passed. Yet in Cana, the finest wine appeared last. This assures us that, under God's blessing, our family story can grow in quality, depth, and sweetness with the passing of time.

Maturity is the fullness that lifts us into a deeper connection, where joy is renewed and strengthened. Hope is the conviction that God honors our willingness to fill the jars each day, transforming our consistency into the seed of a joy that is yet to come.

A Final Reflection

Just as in Cana the miracle occurred after the jars had been filled, many of the deepest transformations in parenting also appear after a long process of consistency.

Sometimes we look back at our story and feel that certain things should have begun earlier. We think about our mistakes, the difficult seasons, or the moments when we did not know how to act. Yet the formation of a child does not depend on a single perfect moment, but on the direction we choose to sustain over time.

Every habit you decide to build, every boundary you maintain with love, every repair you make when something breaks, and every moment you choose to remain connected are jars being filled little by little.

God's grace has the power to take the ordinary and transform it into something new.

That is why hope is not a naive illusion. It is the certainty that, as we walk with intention and faithfulness, God continues to work in the midst of our story.

In Cana, the finest wine did not appear at the beginning of the celebration.

It appeared later.

Parenting follows a similar pattern: over time, consistency, maturity, and grace begin to produce a relationship that is deeper, stronger, and richer in meaning.

The best part of your story is being prepared today.

In Hanna's Universe

Hanna stopped in front of the door to her room.
Her eyes widened in surprise, and her mouth fell
slightly open.
She looked one by one at her faithful
companions.
Dogui had a smile drawn across his face.
Michiko watched with his brow furrowed.
Sagu rested his little paw under his chin, deep in
thought.
They all remembered Mom's last reminder:
—Hanna, don't forget to close the window. The
autumn wind will do its work in your room.
The silence lasted only a moment.
Michiko was the first to speak.
—You should have closed the window.
Dogui was the second. He ran in circles around
the room, dragging the dry leaves scattered across
the floor.
—It's not that bad —he said, wagging his tail—.
We can even have some fun playing with them.
Still surprised, Hanna looked at Sagu.
The little rabbit spoke with his calm voice.
—First we organize the room, and then we finish
the drawing for your homework. We don't have to
do everything in one day, but what's urgent
should be corrected.
Hanna took a deep breath, picked up a leaf from
the floor, and smiled.
—I think today we start by putting things in order.

Hope sustains the process until the fruit appears.

A Note on Influences

This book draws from contributions in developmental psychology, education, and reflections on family formation. Throughout its pages, ideas and perspectives inspired by the work of various authors are woven into the discussion, helping illuminate the emotional development of children and the role adults play in that journey. Among the thinkers who have influenced these reflections are:

Foundations in Attachment and Emotional Development

John Bowlby — Founder of attachment theory, highlighting the central role of secure bonding in a child's emotional development.
Ed Tronick, Ph.D. — Research on emotional communication between parents and children, including the "Still Face Experiment," which demonstrates the importance of connection and relational repair.
Daniel J. Siegel — Interpersonal neurobiology and insights into how relationships shape the developing brain.

Educational Perspectives on Parenting

Alfred Adler and Rudolf Dreikurs — Foundations of positive discipline, belonging, and the child's participation in family life.
Diana Baumrind, Ph.D. — Research on parenting

styles and their influence on children's emotional and social development.

Reflections on Family and Character Formation

James Dobson — Reflections on discipline, connection, and character formation within the family context.
David Hormachea — Perspectives on family health, emotional responsibility, and conflict management.
In addition to these psychological and educational perspectives, this book is also inspired by principles found within the biblical tradition—particularly passages that reflect character formation, wisdom, and the central role of love in family life.
These references are not intended to constitute an exhaustive academic study. Rather, they offer a conceptual framework that helps illuminate the processes described throughout the book.

Notes

Hanna's Universe

A place where families are supported in the emotional, spiritual, and educational growth of children.
Through stories, books, and practical resources, Hanna's Universe helps cultivate meaningful habits, strengthen family connections, and plant seeds of hope in everyday life.
Created by

Rosalina Rangel

Discover more stories and resources at:
www.hannasuniverse.com